MAP WORKBOOK FOR
WORLD HISTORY
VOLUME I: TO 1800

MAP WORKBOOK FOR
WORLD HISTORY

VOLUME I: TO 1800

PREPARED BY
CYNTHIA KOSSO
NORTHERN ARIZONA UNIVERSITY

West/Wadsworth
I(T)P® An International Thomson Publishing Company

Belmont, CA • Albany, NY • Bonn • Boston • Cincinnati • Detroit • Johannesburg • London
Madrid • Melbourne • Mexico City • New York • Paris • Singapore • Tokyo • Toronto • Washington

Printed in the United States of America
1 2 3 4 5 6 7 8 9 10

For more information, contact Wadsworth Publishing Company, 10 Davis Drive, Belmont, CA 94002, or electronically at http://www.thomson.com/wadsworth.html

International Thomson Publishing Europe
Berkshire House 168-173
High Holborn
London, WC1V 7AA, England

International Thomson Editores
Campos Eliseos 385, Piso 7
Col. Polanco
11560 México D.F. México

Thomas Nelson Australia
102 Dodds Street
South Melbourne 3205
Victoria, Australia

International Thomson Publishing Asia
221 Henderson Road
#05-10 Henderson Building
Singapore 0315

Nelson Canada
1120 Birchmount Road
Scarborough, Ontario
Canada M1K 5G4

International Thomson Publishing Japan
Hirakawacho Kyowa Building, 3F
2-2-1 Hirakawacho
Chiyoda-ku, Tokyo 102, Japan

International Thomson Publishing GmbH
Königswinterer Strasse 418
53227 Bonn, Germany

International Thomson Publishing Southern Africa
Building 18, Constantia Park
240 Old Pretoria Road
Halfway House, 1685 South Africa

Senior Developmental Editor: Sharon Adams Poore
Print Buyer: Stacey Weinberger

ISBN 0-534-53126-1

Volume One
TABLE OF CONTENTS

INTRODUCTION

EXERCISES

EXTRA MAPS

INTRODUCTION

The creation of maps has a complex and evolving history. It is a very ancient human activity -- the oldest known map, from ca. 5000 BCE, was found in central Italy carved on a rock overlooking a Neolithic settlement. Another of our earliest existing maps is from the Babylonians in the fifth century BCE. In this map the Babylonians are situated precisely in the middle of the universe, and everything radiates from Babylon. This shows their own, and particularly the map maker's, perception of the world. As the Babylonian map suggests, a human viewpoint as an element in map making is common. [1]

Maps tell us about the physical and cultural aspects of the world, but they can be deceiving. Every map has a point of view or perspective. It has an author (the cartographer), a subject, and a theme. The subject and theme represent the author's interest, but also his or her skills, knowledge of geography, political viewpoints, and historical context. All map makers, therefore, pick a perspective from which to display their particular purpose or orientation, which occasionally is an intentionally false one. Colors, for example, can be and have been used subtly to suggest "good guys" or "bad guys." Countries can be drawn smaller or larger to suggest relative importance. To confuse an "enemy," the map maker may include incorrect details. A world map from the 16th century will show the continents as far as they were known to the Europeans during this age of discovery, but not as we believe them to be today. Any later chart of the Americas will depict the continent as very different in size and shape (clearly, the continents themselves did not change that much). Again, a world map reveals many things about its authors through the selection of details and perspective. In even the most "objective" map, however, one simply cannot add all details in all maps. The map would be rendered incomprehensibly complicated. Thus, it is good to keep in mind that maps do not represent reality, but a version of reality. Maps are like snapshots of the world, a moment in time and space with a definite historical context.

Despite these limitations, there are several basic principles governing the structure and reading of maps, and map reading remains an important part of any person's basic knowledge about the world, whether for travel or keeping track of events around the world. When someone gives you directions, or asks them of you, your brain automatically

---

[1] I would like to thank the undergraduate students, and in particular Clyde Wilson, in the History of Western Civilization courses at Northern Arizona University. They provided indispensable help and advice in the development of this workbook.

attempts to draw a rudimentary map. Your mind may even see roads as lines and rivers as bands or buildings as small squares.

To understand the basic appearance of a map, imagine the world as you see it from an airplane. The very straight lines that you see are generally roads and highways. The winding bands are rivers. Rectangles may be buildings and large dark green masses are forests. Cities are conglomerations of rectangles. If you simply took a picture from your airplane and had it printed you would have a photographic map: a reduced representation of a portion of the surface of the earth. How we see the world from an airplane is, however, somewhat different from how we see it on a map. The world is round. The map page is flat. All map makers, therefore, pick a perspective (as we have seen) and a scale from which to display their particular purpose or orientation.

Since the world is round and most maps are not there is also an unavoidable distortion is the spatial representation of locations. (You may notice that the shapes of continents change slightly from map to map. This is because the distortion is different depending upon the perspective of the map.) Flat maps, however, are not likely to be completely superseded by globes. Carrying a globe on a hike or road trip would be very inconvenient.

In order to make a map (or to read one) a frame of reference is chosen. A grid system within the frame of reference is usually used to help pinpoint locations on the map. In this exercise book, the grid pattern has been removed in order to make the maps less cluttered, but normally the lines of latitude and longitude would be included on the map. These lines appear on most maps you might consult.

Map makers, in order to build a grid system, chose the north and south poles as two definite points from which to begin dividing the world. Midway between these poles a line was drawn around the world (this is the equator). The lines of latitude run parallel to the equator up and down to each pole. The equator provides a natural line from which to measure, but there is no such natural longitude line (but one is put in by convention and is called the prime meridian). A longitudinal starting point is obviously needed as a point of reference. Lines of longitude complete the grid by drawing lines from pole to pole around the planet (the standard one passing through Greenwich, England for historical reasons -- now the commonly accepted prime meridian).

The longitudinal line through Greenwich, England is now used as an accepted reference point, but many nations have, in the past, created maps with their own most important cities as reference points. The United States made maps with Washington DC as the prime meridian. Spain drew it through Madrid, the Greeks through Athens, the Dutch through Amsterdam and so on.

Many different scales of maps are also used. That simply means that there are maps with different proportions between the distance on the map and the actual distance on the world. The larger the fraction (or proportion), the smaller the territory covered. Inches per mile or centimeters per kilometer are the most common kind of scale. The scale is merely a fraction comparing the distances on the map measured in inches or centimeters, with the distances on the ground measured in miles or kilometers (e.g., 1 inch on the map = 10 miles on the ground).

Although the entire process insures that maps will always represent a version of reality, instead of reality itself, maps are becoming more and more accurate. [2] Cartographers have worked to perfect maps since the late middle ages, with much success. This success is our gain, as it enhances our understanding of history, geography, meteorology, cultural and economic distributions of people, ... the list is endless.

That is precisely the purpose of this exercise book -- to help you learn to read and understand maps as well as to help you understand the relation between places and people through time. The maps will help you order events and historical locations. Nearly all exercises incorporate three parts. There is a brief introduction to each exercise. The section marked "locations" asks you to find and correctly place on the map provided cities, boundaries and other features. The "questions" section asks you to attempt to relate, or synthesize, the historical and geographical information that you have absorbed.

BRIEF BIBLIOGRAPHY

Demko, George with Jerome Agel and Eugene Boe. 1992. *Why in the World, Adventures in Geography*. New York: Doubleday. This is a fun and easy to read introduction to mapping and geography. It does an excellent job of pointing out the importance of geography.

Greenhood, David. 1964. *Mapping*. Chicago: University of Chicago Press. This book provides a clear and concise introduction to maps and mapping.

Wood, Denis. 1992. *The Power of Maps*. New York: The Guilford Press. In this book Wood shows how maps are used and abused. It is an excellent introduction to the way maps have been used by groups and individuals to make an argument or present a point of view.

---

[2]The 1993, <u>Hammond, Atlas of the World</u>, is a beautiful example of this trend.

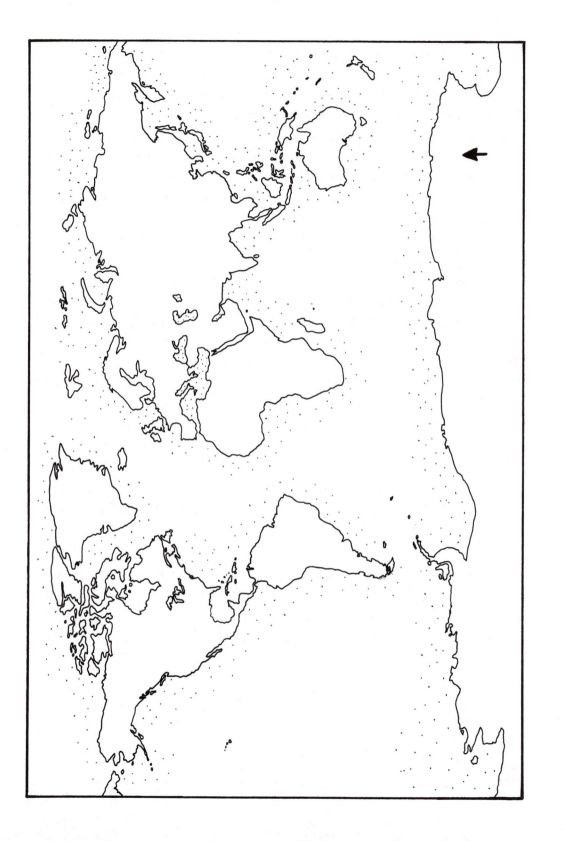

Exercise 1
The World: Major Regions

Introduction

This exercise puts into perspective the major regions of the planet, as we know them today. Civilizations developed in a world context. They were not, and are not, isolated entities. Interactions among the various regions and people are evident from very early in human history. People traded with one another for food, tools and raw materials. In that process, they learned about one another, sometimes adopting practices, sometimes improving upon the technologies and customs that they found.

The earliest civilizations were found worldwide, in the hills and valleys of Mesoamerica, the Fertile Crescent, India, China and Egypt.

Locations

With different colored pencils, shade or draw in and label the following regions and geographical features. You may number the locations and place the numbers on the map for clarity.

A. Regions	11. Japan	22. Rhine	32. Pacific Ocean
1. Anatolia	12. North Africa	23. Tigris	33. Persian Gulf
2. Arabia	13. North America	24. Yangtze	34. Red Sea
3. Australia	14. Russia		
4. Balkan	15. South America	**C. Seas, Oceans,**	**D. Mountains**
Peninsula	16. Southeast Asia	**Lakes**	35. Alps
5. Britain		25. Atlantic Ocean	36. Caucasus
6. China	**B. Rivers**	26. Black Sea	37. Himalayan
7. Egypt	17. Amazon	27. Caribbean	Mts.
8. Fertile Crescent	18. Danube	28. Great Lakes	38. Pyrennes
9. Iberian	19. Ganges	29. Indian Ocean	39. Rockies
Peninsula	20. Mississippi	30. Mediterranean	40. Taurus
10. Iran	21. Nile	31. North Sea	

Questions

In some ways, the development of civilizations remains a mystery. What are some of the theories used to explain their existence? What advantages and disadvantages do civilizations offer to us as human beings?

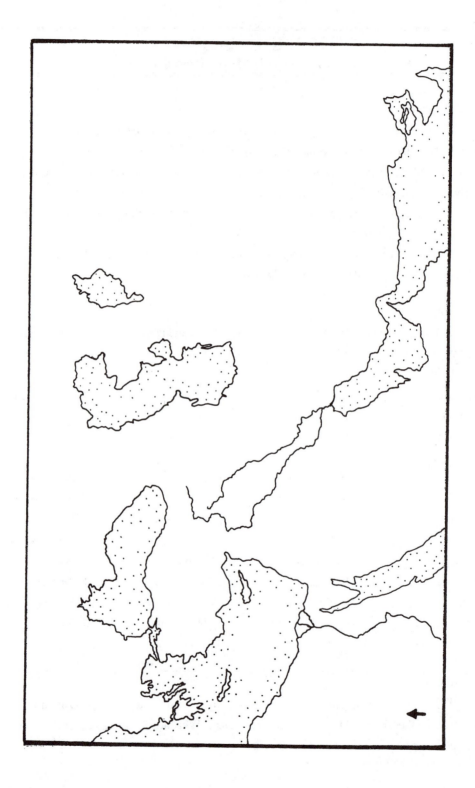

Exercise 2
Ancient People and Political Boundaries of the Near East

Introduction

Mesopotamia, Greek for the "land between the rivers," was a rich land but difficult to farm. It took cooperation to build the irrigation systems needed to produce large quantities of agricultural goods. It was here that some of the earliest precursors to civilization were born. Writing, science, organized religion, and advanced technologies were a part of civilizations that arose in Mesopotamia.

In fact, one the earliest world maps still in existence is on a cuneiform tablet from the Babylonians. It is elementary and may have been a school book exercise, but it suggests that even as early as 500 BCE, the Babylonians saw that they were part of a larger whole that included both a round earth (with Babylon at the center) and the surrounding heavens. In this exercise you will locate some of the important empires in the Near East and Egypt.

Locations

With different colored pencils, label the following cities and regions and carefully draw in the imperial boundaries at their greatest extent. There will be overlap of some boundaries.

A. Empires

1. Assyrian
2. Chaldean
3. Egyptian
4. Hittite
5. Persian

B. Regions

6. Akkad

7. Asia Minor
8. Assyria
9. Lower Egypt
10. Mesopotamia
11. Nile Delta
12. Palestine
13. Parthia
14. Sinai
15. Sumer

16. Syria
17. Upper Egypt

C. Cities

18. Babylon
19. Jerusalem
20. Thebes

Questions

What are the dates of the Hittite, Egyptian, Assyrian and Persian Empires? What factors enabled the Assyrians and then the Persians to control such vast tracts of territory? What attracted these groups to the shores of the Mediterranean? What were the strengths of the Assyrians? What were the goals of the Persians?

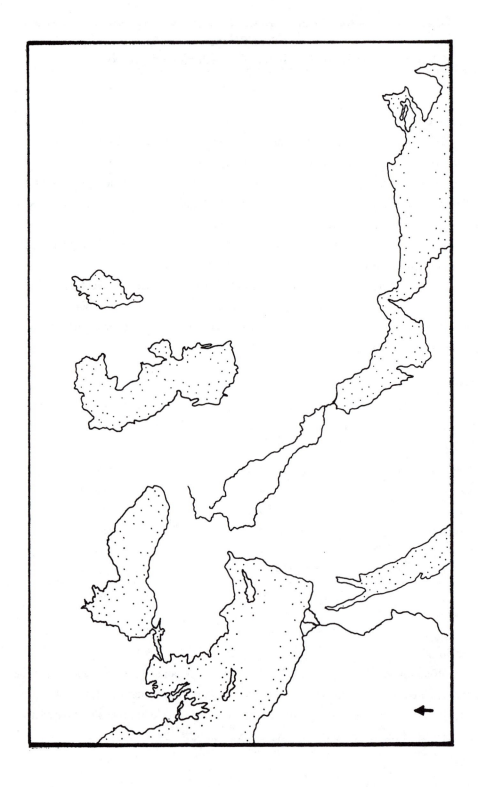

Exercise 3
Major Cities of the Ancient Near East and Egypt

Introduction

From the Near East and Egypt we get some of the earliest complex civilizations, with organized religion, public works projects, and writing. The Hebrews, a small tribe of people, provide the western world with a spiritual heritage out of proportion to their size. The "Fertile Crescent" was fertile for more than agricultural products. It was fertile ground, as well, for political, cultural and religious ideas.

Small states gave way to empires and these gave way to new states and imperial systems. These states grew up around cities. The Near East and Egypt are home to some of the oldest urban centers on earth. This exercise introduces you to some of these early cities.

Locations

Label the following Near Eastern and Egyptian cities on the map provided. On your map please add the approximate foundation dates, whenever possible, of each of these cities:

1. Abu Simbel	8. Jerico	15. Tel el Amarna
2. Assur	9. Jerusalem	16. Thebes
3. Babylon	10. Lagash	17. Tyre
4. Çatal Hüyük	11. Luxor	18. Umma
5. Eridu	12. Memphis	19. Ur
6. Gaza	13. Nineveh	20. Uruk
7. Giza	14. Nippur	

Questions

From your reading describe the physical environment of these sites. How did this environment affect the beliefs of the settlers at Çatal Hüyük, Babylon, and Thebes? What were some of their beliefs about the world?

Exercise 4
China in Antiquity

Introduction

Ancient Chinese civilization began to emerge about 5,000 years ago along the Yellow and the Yangtze rivers. In the middle of the first millenium, territorial warfare had become endemic, but by the third century BCE, China had become a real empire and a dominant cultural and political force -- as it remains today. This exercise considers some of the major geographical regions, cultural regions andwarring states of early China.

Locations

With different colored pencils, shade in and label the following cities, geographical features, regions and imperial boundaries

A. Cities

1. Anyang

2. Changan

3. Luoyang

4. Zhengzhou

B. Geographical features

5. Gobi Desert

6. Huai River

7. Pacific Ocean

8. South China Sea

9. Tibetan Plateau

10. Yangtze River

11. Yellow River

12. Yellow Sea

C. Warring states

13. Jin

14. Qin

15. Song

16. Wu

17. Yen

D. Empires and regions

18. Han Empire

19. Shang Regions

20. Zhou Royal Domain

Questions

Why are the two great rivers (Yellow and Yangtze) considered the core regions in the development of Chinese civilization?

In what ways was the development of this eastern civilization the same, and in what ways was it different, from contemporaries in other parts of the world (e.g. Mesopotamia)?

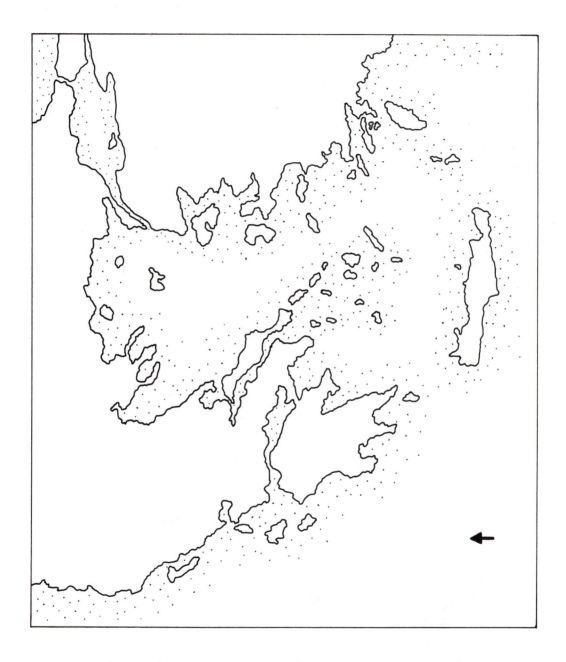

Exercise 5
The Geography and Regions of Ancient Greece

Introduction

Throught-out much of its history, the world of the ancient Greeks was divided up into many small politically independent states. Geography, especially the mountains and the sea, played a vital role in the way Greek political and social systems developed. This exercise is intended to familiarize you with the main regions and geographical features of the Greek peninsula.

Locations

With different colored pencils, shade in and label the following regions and geographical features and major cities.

A. Regions	9. Thrace	16. Propontis
1. Attica		17. Sea of Crete
2. Boeotia	**B. Bodies of water**	
3. Crete	10. Adriatic Sea	**C. Mountains**
4. Ionia	11. Aegean Sea	18. Mt. Olympus
5. Laconia	12. Gulf of Corinth	19. Mt. Parnassus
6. Macedonia	13. Hellespont	20. Mt. Taygetos
7. Peloponnesus	14. Ionian Sea	
8. Thessaly	15. Mediterranean	

Questions

Describe the geography of Greece. What role did geography play in the evolution of Greek history? How does the environment of Greece compare to that of Egypt and the Near East? What advantages and what disadvantages did the Greeks have because of their location?

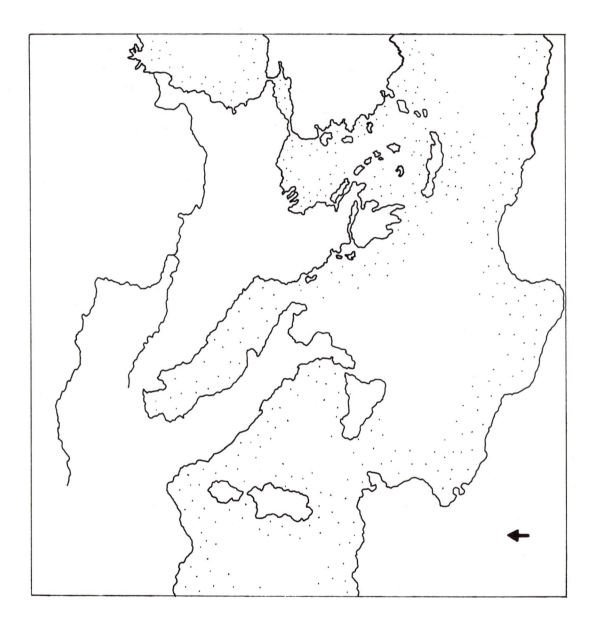

Exercise 6
The World of Classical Greece

Introduction

The world of the Greeks was much larger than the main peninsula of Greece. It stretched from Asia Minor to Italy, and beyond. The islands of the Cyclades, which form a rough circle coming off the tip of Euboea and Attica, were inhabited very early. They were politically important for resources, strategy and religion. Melos was the only local source of obsidian for weapons and surgical instruments. Delos was the home of Apollo and was sacred. On Crete an early civilization flourished for more than a thousand years. Mainland Greeks were influenced by the Cretans and used and depended upon the political and economic support of these island people.

In the west the Greeks quickly saw the value in the lands of Italy, settling there and spreading Greek cultural and technological ideas into the west. In this exercise some of the main regions, cities and islands of the Greek world are located.

Locations

With different colored pencils, shade in and label the following cities, islands and regions.

A. Cities and sites	9. Olympia	B. Islands	24. Samos
1. Argos	10. Pella	16. Amorgos	
2. Athens	11. Sparta	17. Corcyra	C. Regions
3. Corinth	12. Syracuse	18. Crete	25. Attica
4. Delphi	13. Tarentum	19. Euboea	26. Boeotia
5. Eretria	14. Thebes	20. Lesbos	27. Laconia
6. Knossos	15. Troy	21. Melos	28. Macedonia
7. Marathon		22. Naxos	29. Magna Graecia
8. Miletus		23. Rhodes	30. Thrace

Questions

The Greeks were rarely a quietly settled people. Which were the areas most colonized by the Greeks. When did the colonization movement begin? Why? Try to explain why the Greeks chose to colonize where they did.

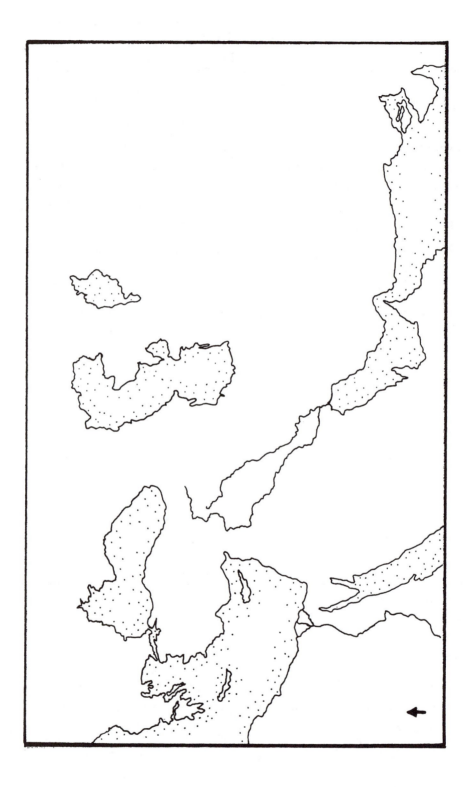

Exercise 7
The Cities and Monarchies of the Hellenistic world

Introduction

Alexander the Great changed the political map of the "civilized" world. His ambitions led him to conquer his neighbors on the Balkan peninsula and then head to the east. He incorporated dozens of cultures and thousands of miles into his Macedonian Empire. The creation of this empire was hard won, but not long lasting. Upon Alexander's untimely death, his conquests were divided among his faithful generals. The following exercise traces Alexander's conquests and the territorial divisions that occurred after his death.

Locations

With different colored pencils, carefully shade in and label the following cities and battle sites of the Hellenistic world. Also outline the boundaries of the monarchies and leagues. There will be overlap of boundaries.

A. Cities	9. Gaza	B. Battle sites	20. Aetolian
1. Alexandria	10. Memphis	16. Gaugamela	League
2. Antioch	11. Pella	17. Granicus River	21. Alexander's
3. Athens	12. Persepolis	18. Issus	Empire
4. Babylon	13. Sparta		22. Antigonid
5. Bactra	14. Susa	C. Monarchies	23. Pergamene
6. Cyrene	15. Tyre	and leagues	24. Ptolemaic
7. Damascus		19. Achaean	25. Seleucid
8. Ephesus		League	

Questions

What factors contributed to the successful campaigns of Alexander the Great? What were the long term effects of Alexander's conquests on the areas that he captured? The kingdoms that replaced Alexander's monarchy, created several centuries of relative stability, but these kingdoms were never able to enforce peace. Why not?

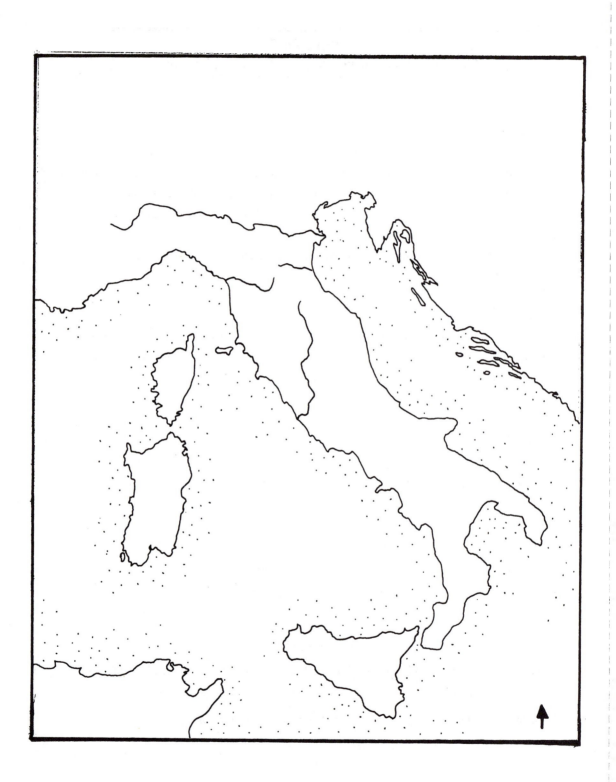

Exercise 8
The Geography and Cities of Ancient Italy

Introduction

From a small village on a hill overlooking the Tiber river, Rome grew into one of the most powerful states in Western History. The Romans, moreover, forged one of the world's longest lived imperial systems -- in ancient or modern history. The Italian peninsula was the first territory to come under the control of these powerful people. This exercise is an introduction to some of the early cities, regions and geographical features of Italy.

Locations

With different colored pencils, mark and label the following cities, regions and geographical features.

A. Cities	B. Regions	C. Geographical features
1. Brindisi	8. Corsica	14. Adriatic Sea
2. Messina	9. Etruria	15. Apennine Mountains
3. Naples	10. Latium	16. Arno River
4. Rome	11. Magna Graecia	17. Ionian Sea
5. Syracuse	12. Sardinia	18. Po River
6. Tarentum	13. Sicily	19. Rubicon River
7. Veii		20. Tiber River

Questions

Several groups had significant impact on the Romans. Who were these people and what did they contribute to the development of Roman culture and politics?

What areas in Italy provided the best agricultural land? What other resources did the peninsula provide for the Italians? Compare the geography of Italy to the Greek peninsula. What advantages did Italy possess over Greece and how did this affect their respective histories?

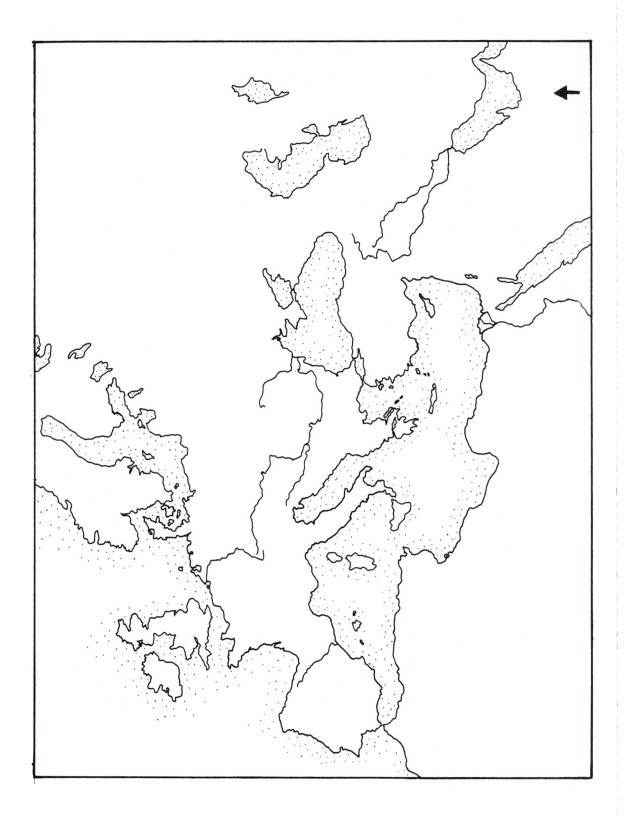

Exercise 9
The Roman Republican Conquest of the Mediterranean

Introduction

After the conquest of the Italian peninsula, the Romans began to interact forcefully with their more distant neighbors. Beginning in the Western Mediterranean, the Romans gained territory rapidly. External conflict was inevitable in their expansion. Among the most famous of all the wars fought by the Romans were the Punic, or Carthaginian, wars. One of the greatest Carthaginian generals was Hannibal -- among the few who attacked the Romans on their own territory in these early days of Roman growth.

Of course, Rome's social and political institutions had difficulties keeping up with the changes and there were some internal upheavals. Nevertheless, the Romans managed to forge a strong and enduring political system. This exercise traces the growth of the Roman Republican empire and the progress of the Second Punic War.

Locations

With colored pencils, trace the growth of the western Mediterranean empire. Outline the following boundaries, routes and place the number of the following locations on the map.

A. Boundaries and Routes	B. Sites and regions	
1. Boundary of western empire ca. 31 BCE.	3. Africa (Carthage)	7. Numidia
	4. Cannae	8. Sardinia
2. Hannibal's route during the Second Punic War	5. Cisalpine Gaul	9. Sicily
	6. Lake Trasimene	10. Spain

Questions

Why were the Romans interested in the western Mediterranean? The eastern? What advantage did the control of these regions offer to the Romans? What were the main natural and man-made resources from Spain, Greece, Egypt, Sicily, and Northern Africa?

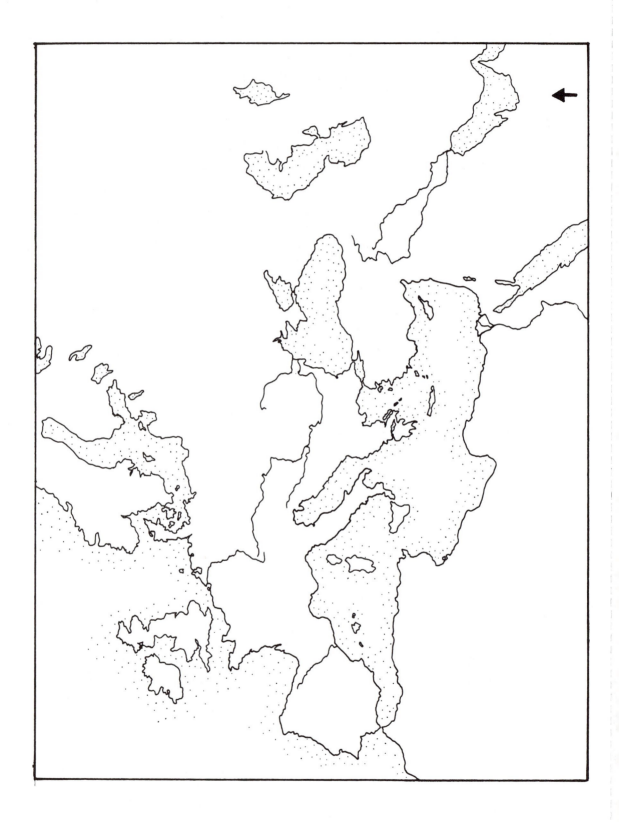

Exercise 10
The Roman Empire

Introduction

The Romans continued to expand their lands after the Imperial system of government was in place. New territories were needed to bring in more income. As regions were added to the empire, the need for an efficient and regulated administration grew. Wisely, and whenever possible, the Romans co-opted existing systems of management. The Roman approach to control of subject people tended to smooth the transition to membership in the Empire and reduced the chances of rebellion and dissatisfaction.

Locations

With different colored pencils, number and trace the following boundaries and provinces on your map.

A. Boundaries

1. Draw, with a dotted line, the boundary of the Roman Empire at 14 CE.

2. Using a solid line, add the boundary of the Roman Empire at its height in 117 CE.

B. Provinces of the second century

3. Britain

4. Judaea

5. Macedonia

6. Africa

7. Egypt

8. Dacia

9. Spain

10. Illyria

Questions

What new provinces were added by the second century CE? Which were lost and which remained in the restored Empire of the third century CE?

Cities were important for the administration of the Roman imperial government. What were the names of three of the largest cities in the Roman empire? What were the estimated populations of these cities? Why were cities so important to the Romans? Describe the functions that they served. Were there differences between the cities of the eastern and the western parts of the empire? If so, what were the differences?

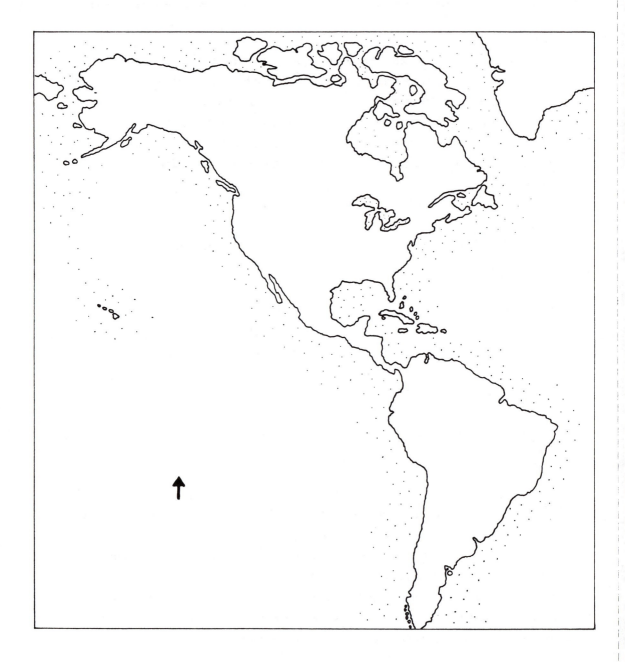

Exercise 11
The Early Americas

Introduction

The Americas have long been inhabited by humans, but just how long is a matter of continued debate (perhaps from about 15,000 years ago). It is clear, however, that by the second millennium before the present era, highly organized societies had appeared in Central and South America. The civilizations that grew out of the smaller societies were characterized by vast trade networks, hierarchical political structures, written language, monumental architecture and stunning and vivid artworks. This exercise is a brief introduction to the region and its major early kingdoms.

Locations

With different colored pencils, shade in and label the following geographic features. Then using different colored pencils mark the boundaries of the following chiefdoms, states or empires. Lastly, lightly shade in and number the areas where farming people had located in both North and South America.

A. Geographic features

1. Amazon River
2. Andes Mountains
3. Atlantic Ocean
4. Caribbean Sea
5. Gulf of Mexico

B. Chiefdoms, states or empires

6. Aztec

7. Inca
8. Maya
9. North Andean Chiefdoms

C. North American people

10. Desert gatherers
11. Plains hunters
12. Plateau fishermen
13. Pueblo Indians
14. Sub arctic hunters

15. Woodlnd farmers

D. South American people

16. Farming tribes
17. Maize and manioc cultivators
18. Maritime hunters
19. Savannah farmers
20. Steppe hunters

Questions

The civilizations of the Americas developed in relative isolation from the rest of the world -- undisturbed until the arrival of Columbus and the Spanish. What were the advantages and disadvantages of this isolation? What were some of the most remarkable cultural achievements made by the people of the Americas?

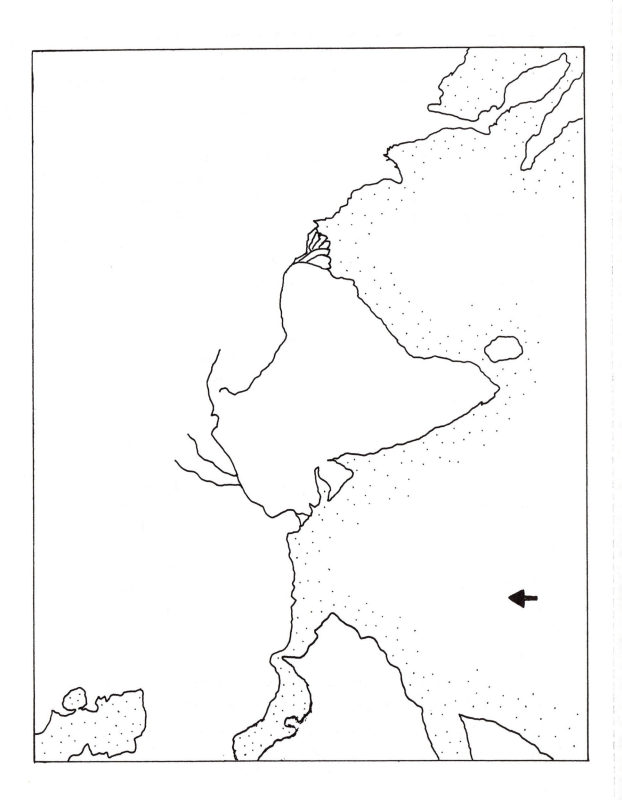

Exercise 12
India: Ancient and Medieval

Introduction

In the last centuries before the modern era, the people of India were divided into several kingdoms and states. Not until about the second century BCE did stable kingdoms arise. The Gupta and Chola kingdoms were able to remain in power for centuries at a time. India functioned as an economic and physical link between east and west. This economic security, coupled with relative political stability, contributed to the flowering of Indian culture and religion. Even the scarce records of the Gupta testify to Indian cultural greatness. In the middle ages, Islam began to compete with indigenous Hindu beliefs. Conflict between Hindu and Moslem began, and continues to disrupt Indian politics to this day.

Locations

On the map provided locate the following ancient sites, cities, regions and geographical features.

A. Sites	11. Topra	**C. Regions/**	24. Surashtra
1. Bairat		**states**	25. Tibet
2. Champa	**B. Cities**	17. Asoka empire,	
3. Gimar	10. Benares	250 BCE	**D. Geographical**
4. Harrappa	11. Bodh Gaya	18. Chalukyas	**features**
5. Jaugada	12. Delhi	19. Cholas	26. Arabian Sea
6. Kalsi	13. Kanchi	20. Cola kingdom	27. Bay of Bengal
7. Mohenjo-Dara	14. Lahore	21. Gupta dynasty,	28. Ganges River
8. Rummindi	15. Nellore	320 BCE	29. Himalayan
9. Shahbazgarhi	16. Samarkand	22. Kashmir	Mts.
10. Siddapura		23. Magadha	30. Indus River

Questions

How did the coming of Islam affect the government of the Indian states? What were the main consequences of the conflict of values inherent in the meeting of two different systems of belief?

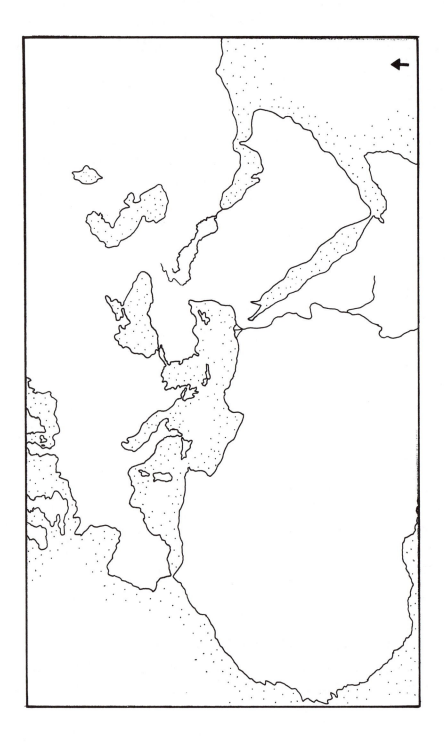

Exercise 13
The Expansion of Islam

Introduction

In the seventh century Arab tribes began to accept a new religion, Islam, and to expand their influence in both the eastern and western Mediterranean world. The acceptance of Islam by the Arabs was rapid and complete. The reasons for such a rapid and successful religious revolution are still not clear.

Upon unifying politically, as well as religiously, the Arabs began to expand their territory. This exercise traces the spread of Islamic power and influence across Northern Africa and up through the Near East and beyond.

Locations

With a different colored marking pencils carefully draw the boundaries of the following empires and Islamic territories at and after Muhammed's death. There will be overlap. Place thenumber of the following cities and regions on your map.

A. Cities

1. Alexandria

2. Antioch

3. Baghdad

4. Constantinople

5. Cordoba

6. Mecca

7. Medina

8. Poitiers

9. Tripoli

10. Tunis

B. Regions

11. Arabia

12. Sahara Desert

13. Egypt

C. Boundaries and Empires

14. Abbasid Caliphate

15. Byzantine Empire

16. Islamic territories at 632

17. Islamic territories at 661

18. Islamic territories at 750

19. Persian Empire

20. Sassasian Empire

Questions

What factors enabled the expansion of Islam on such a large scale? What factors stopped the expansion into Christian Europe? What impact did the Islamic conquests have on Christian Europe?

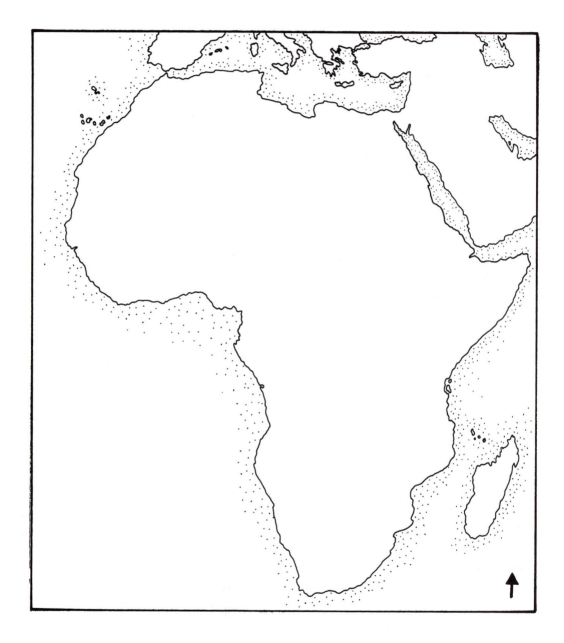

Exercise 14
Ancient Africa

Introduction

Africa is the second largest continent on earth, was home to the earliest hominids, the immediate ancestors to modern man, and arguably the site of the earliest cultivation of plants and domestication of animals (in Nubia). In North Africa, Egypt has long been recognized as one of the world's greatest and earliest complex civilizations. Elsewhere in Africa, however, populous and complex states also appeared. A vast variety of people inhabited the continent and Africa provided an environment which inspired the creation of several distinct civilizations and kingdoms. This exercise introduces you to some of these people, their states, and some major geographical features.

Locations

On the map, label the following cities or settlements, people, regions, kingdoms and geographical features.

A. Cities and settlements	B. People	15. Ethiopia	21. Cape of Good Hope
1. Adulis	9. Berbers	16. Kingdom of Kush	22. Cape Verde
2. Axum	10. Ghana	17. Madagascar	23. Congo River
3. Carthage	11. Hausa	18. Nubia	24. Indian Ocean
4. Marrakech	12. Khoisan		25. Mediterranean
5. Meroe	C. Regions and kingdoms	D. Geographical features	26. Niger River
6. Mombassa			27. Nile River
7. Thebes	13. Congo (or Kongo)	19. Atlantic Ocean	28. Red Sea
8. Timbuktu		20. Blue Nile	29. Sahara Desert
	14. Egypt		30. Zambezi River

Questions

Describe the locations and uses of the Iron Age sites found on the African continent. What seems to have motivated people to live in these particular areas? What advantages and disadvantages would they have found in their environments?

Briefly discuss the connections between the kingdoms of Kush, Axum and the western trading states. What kinds of items were exchanged? What were the long term results of this trading activity?

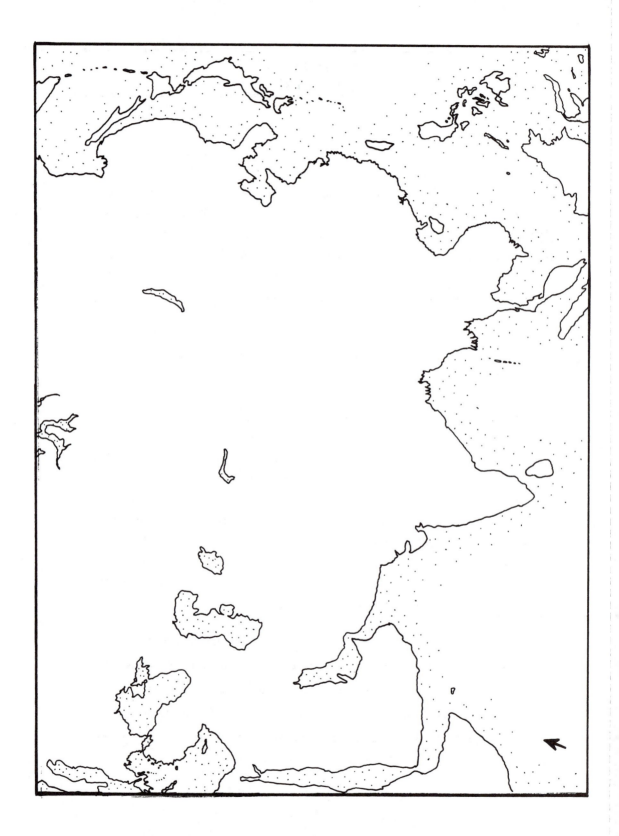

Exercise 15
The Mongols

Introduction

The Mongols came out of the east so quickly and so successfully the Europeans could only pray for their salvation. The Russians were essentially defenseless against them. The Chinese and other people of Asia were under their yoke by the early thirteenth century. These nomadic people had set out to conquer the world and very nearly managed it. This exercise shows the extent of their empire, which lasted several centuries.

Locations

With different colored pencils, locate and draw in the following khanates, regions, geographical features and cities.

A. Khanates

1. Khanate of Chagadai
2. Khanate of Kipchak
3. Khanate of Persia
4. Khanate of the Great
   Khan

B. Regions

5. Afghanistan
6. Arabia
7. Burma
8. India
9. Mesopotamia

10. Mongolia
11. Persia
12. Siberia
13. Vietnam

C. Geographical features

14. Arabian Sea
15. Bay of Bengal
16. Ganges River
17. Persian Gulf
18. Red Sea
19. Tigris River
20. Yellow River

D. Cities

21. Baghdad
22. Bakhara
23. Calicut
24. Canton
25. Cittagong
26. Hormuz
27. Kiev
28. Lhasa
29. Mecca
30. Moscow

Questions

What factors allowed the Mongols to control such vast tracts of territory so quickly? What were their main strengths? What were their motivations? Why did the Mongols fail to take over western Europe? How did the Mongols treat their subjects? What long term effects did the Mongols have on the territories and people that they conquered and then controlled?

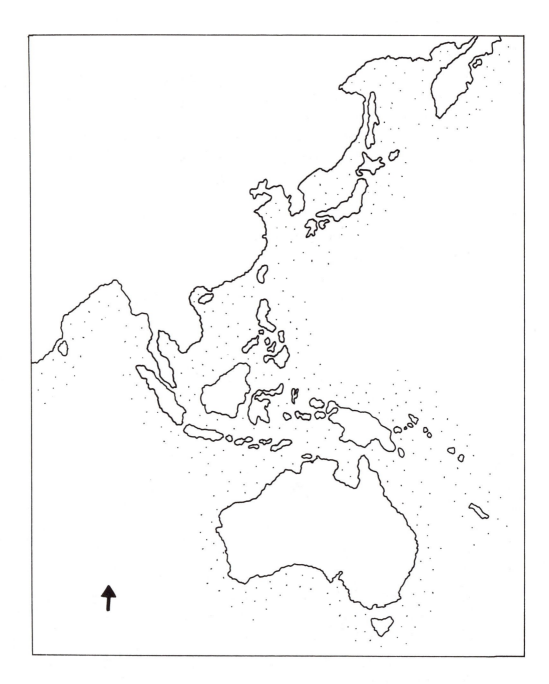

Exercise 16
Early East Asian Rimlands

Introduction

Japan was inhabited from very early times. Though not at first as technologically skilled as its large neighbor to the east, China, the Japanese would create a vital, politically independent and culturally distinct society -- as it remains to today.

This exercise introduces you to Japan and its neighbors.

Locations

With different colored pencils, shade in and label the following cities, geographical features and regions

A. Cities

1. E d o
2. Hangzhou
3. Hanoi
4. Kyoto
5. Nara
6. Nagasaki
7. Pyongyang

B. Geographical features

8. Gobi Desert
9. Huai River
10. Pacific Ocean

11. South China Sea
12. Yangtze River
13. Yellow River
14. Yellow Sea

C. Regions

15. China
16. Hokkaido
17. Japan
18. Korea
19. Okinawa
20. Shikoko

Questions

What role did geography play in the development of Japan? How does Japan's geographic environment differ from China's? What are the advantages and disadvantages of the Japanese environment?

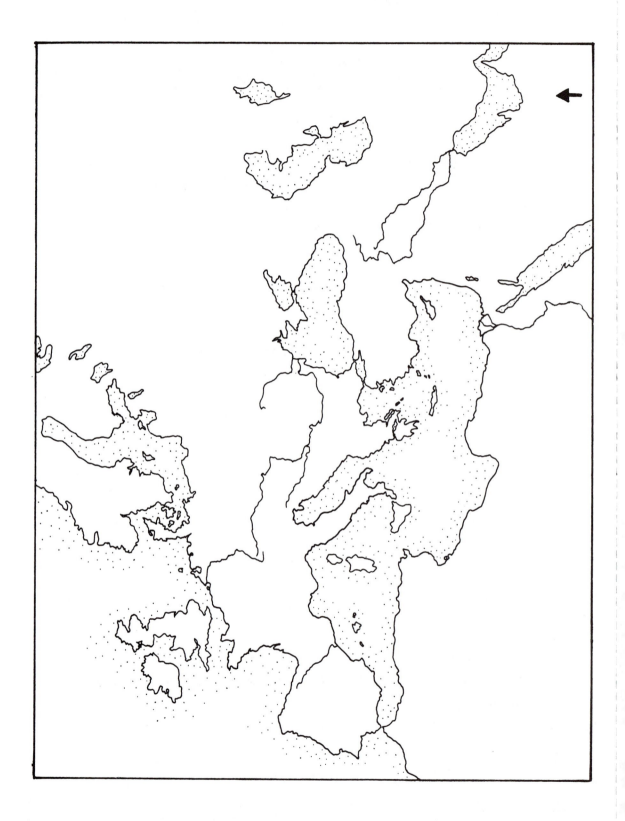

Exercise 17
The Territories of Byzantium

Introduction

While in the west the Roman system was slowly taken over by Germanic peoples, in the eastern half of the old Roman Empire the government remained stable and powerful. This eastern Roman Empire has become known as the Byzantine Empire, though the inhabitants continued to think of themselves as "Roman." The emperors of the east considered the Germans in the west merely as regents of Roman power. In the sixth century, however, a real attempt was made to reunite the old empire into a territorial and institutional whole. The Emperor Justinian was the mastermind behind this plan, and he was partially and temporarily successful.

Locations

Using different colored pencils trace the boundaries of the Byzantine Empire listed below and outline the territories of Byzantium's neighbors.

A. Boundaries

1. Byzantine Empire under Emperor Justinian

(shade in those areas conquered by Justinian)

2. Byzantine territory in the eighth century CE.

B. Byzantium's neighbors

3. Arabs

4. Bulgars

5. Burgundians

6. Franks

7. Ostrogoths

8. Persians

9. Vandals

10. Visigoths

Questions

What territories had Justinian gained for the Byzantines? How were these territories later lost? What were the main characteristics of the empire in the eighth century?

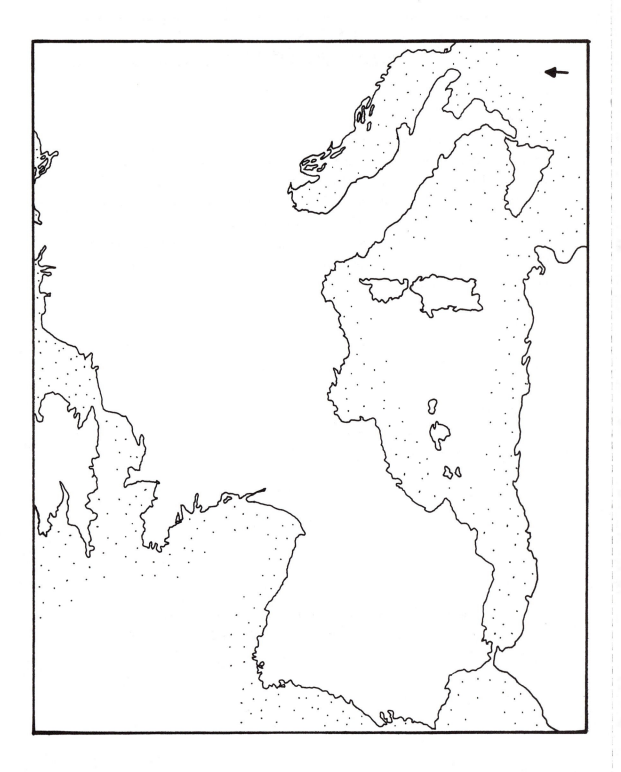

Exercise 18
The Carolingian Empire

Introduction

The Frankish (Merovingian) kingdom controlled the old Roman province of Gaul for several centuries. This was a united Christian kingdom. By the seventh century, however, the kingdom was divided and beginning to weaken. Charles Martel, the mayor of the palace of Austrasia, gained power as a result. Among the most important of his actions was the defeat of the Muslims at Poitiers. But it was his son, Pepin, who, with the help of the Catholic church, would depose the Merovingians formally. Thus a new Frankish kingdom was born -- that of the Carolingians. The son of Pepin, Charlemagne (or Charles the Great), was the most renowned and powerful of the leaders of the Carolingians.

This exercise traces the conquests of Charlemagne and the divisions of the kingdom after his death.

Locations

With different colored pencils draw and label the boundaries, territories and cities of the Carolingians as noted below.

A. Territories

1. Carolingian empire at 768 CE
2. Boundary of the Carolingian empire after the
   conquests of Charlemagne
3. Kingdom of Louis
4. Kingdom of Lothair
5. Kingdom of Charles

B. Cities

6. Aachen

7. Barcelona
8. Bordeaux
9. Cologne
10. Lyons
11. Mainz
12. Milan
13. Paris
14. Rome
15. Verdun

Questions

What were the long term results of the Treaty of Verdun? Describe the differences that were emerging in the divided territories of the Carolingian Empire. What nations would replace the Carolingian territories?

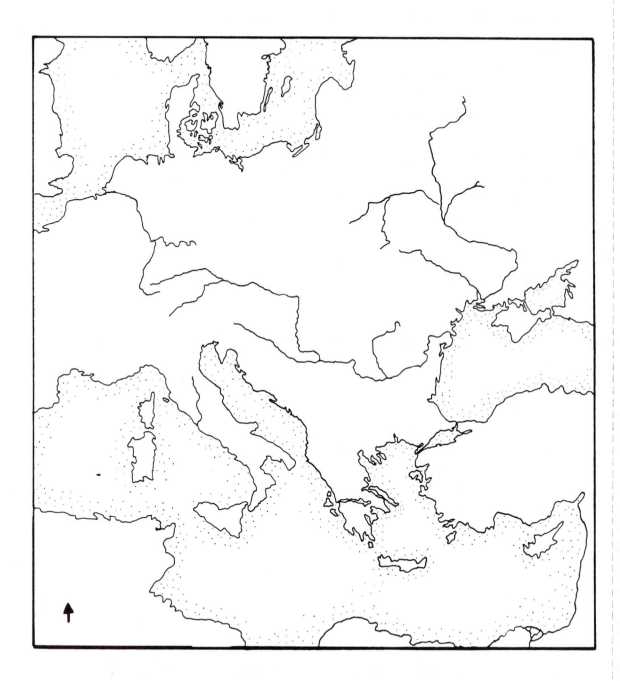

Exercise 19
The Boundaries of Northern and Eastern Europe

Introduction

Many of the countries in northern Europe had little stable political organization until about CE 1000, when Denmark, Sweden and Norway developed complex political structures. In eastern Europe there was much expansion and contraction -- and disagreement -- over boundaries. Around the territories on each side of the Oder river, there was considerable intermixing of German with Slav, which resulted unstable Polish borders. This intermixing of people is a characteristic that has caused disputes in Poland well into the twentieth century.

Locations

With different colored pencils, locate and draw in the following kingdoms, countries, people, cities, and rivers.

A. Kingdoms	8. Sweden	**D. Cities**
1. Holy Roman Empire		14. Belgrade
2. Kingdom of Rus	**C. People**	15. Cracow
3. Kingdom of Sicily	9. Bulgarians	16. Kiev
	10. Croats	17. Vienna
B. Countries	11. Danes	
4. Hungary	12. Prussians	**E. Rivers**
5. Norway	13. Serbs	18. Danube River
6. Poland		19. Dniester River
7. Pomerania		20. Vistula River

Questions

List at least five of the major regions of the Holy Roman Empire. Try to offer an explanation for these divisions of the Holy Roman Empire. Did they help or hinder stability in the Empire? Explain.

Why did the boundaries of the eastern European countries tend to shift? Can these shifts be compared to modern day eastern Europe? Describe any modern conflicts over boundaries in these regions.

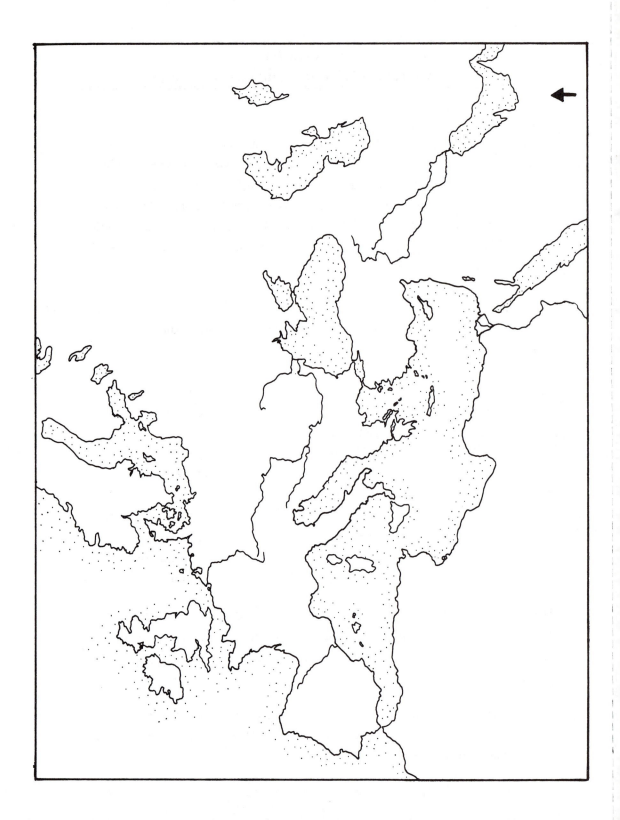

Exercise 20
The Black Death

Introduction

The Black Death was a disaster of enormous magnitude. It killed between 25% to 50% of the population of Europe. In some cases entire villages were wiped out. Some cities saw their populations reduced by more than half.

The inhabitants of Europe responded to this disaster in a variety of inventive ways -- not all of them pleasant. The disaster had far reaching cultural, economic and religious results.

Locations

On your map, using different colored pencils, trace the progression of the Black Death and locate the following cities:

A. The Black Death, draw the boundaries of the disease in	7. Dec. 1350	14. Hamburg
		15. London
	B. Cities	16. Messina
1. 1347	8. Aachen	17. Milan
2. June 1348	9. Berlin	18. Paris
3. Dec. 1348	10. Cologne	19. Rome
4. June 1349	11. Copenhagen	20. York
5. Dec. 1349	12. Dublin	
6. June 1350	13. Durham	

Questions

Discuss the responses to the Black Death. What were some of the psychological and religious responses experienced by the inhabitants of Europe? Did the people of all regions act in similar or different ways? Give specific examples. What economic ramifications did the Black Death have? Be fairly detailed. Do you think that the Black Death had long term effects? Defend your answer.

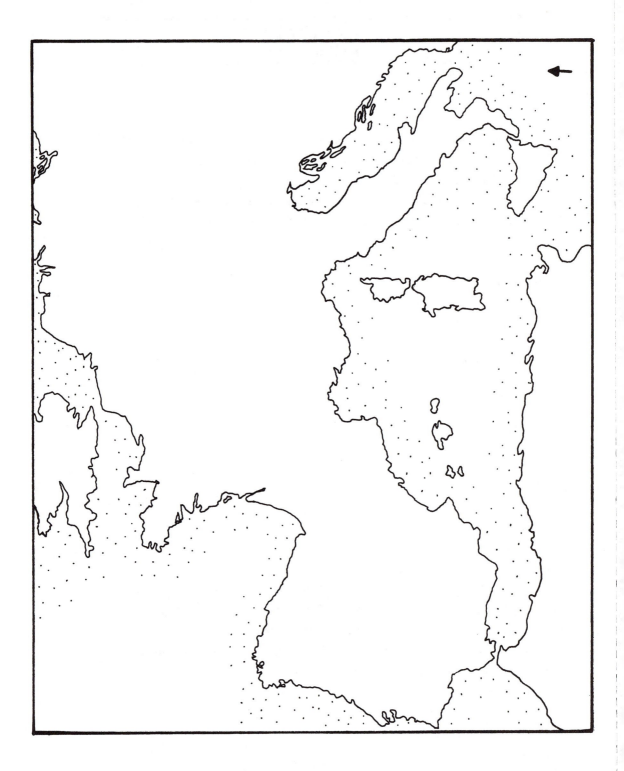

Exercise 21
South-western Europe: 14th-15th Century Political Divisions

Introduction

By the fourteenth century Italy had a well established system of city-state governments, often in conflict with one another. The stronger usually snatching the territories of the weaker. By the fifteenth century there were only a few, very powerful states left. They vied with one another for a variety of reasons, often calling on the Papacy or the Holy Roman Empire of the Germans to support their claims. Frequent warfare was the result, and unification of Italy was a long way away.

Spain was home to several independent Christian nations that had managed, together, to recover the peninsula from those practicing Islam-- in particular -- and Judaism. The Spanish enforced strict orthodoxy. Unlike the leaders and states of Italy, Isabella of Castile and Ferdinand of Aragon made major progress toward early unification of the Iberian peninsula. Their combined power and wealth, plus the support of the Catholic Church, made them a real threat to countries near and far. This exercise considers the territories and states of both Spain and Italy.

Locations

With different colored pencils, draw in and number the following political boundaries and cities.

A. Boundaries -- Italy	5. Papal States	B. Boundaries -- Iberian Peninsula	C. Cities
1. Duchy of Ferrara	6. Republic of Florence	9. Aragon	14. Barcelona
	7. Republic of Siena	10. Castile	15. Genoa
2. Duchy of Milan		11. Granada	16. Madrid
3. Duchy of Savoy	8. Republic of Venice	12. Navarre	17. Milan
		13. Portugal	18. Naples
4. Kingdom of Naples			19. Toledo
			20. Venice

Questions

Name the five major powers in Italy during the fifteenth century. How did these powers come to dominate? Why weren't they stable and peaceful? Additionally, try to explain the emergence of the independent Christian states on the Iberian peninsula. Who unified these states?

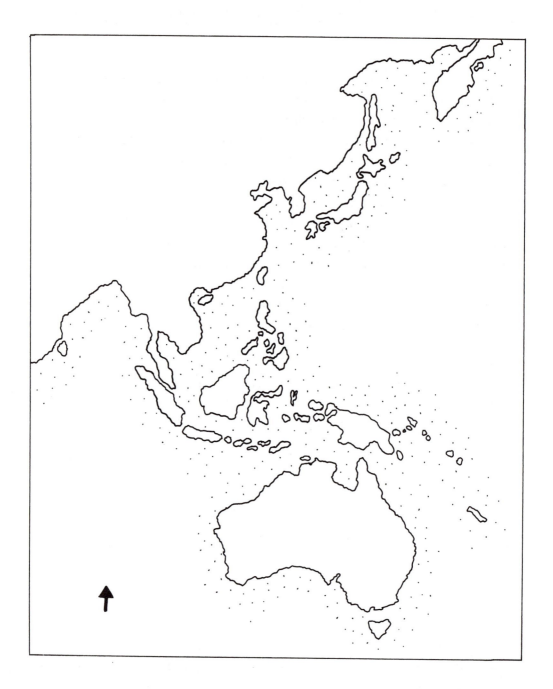

Exercise 22
Southeast Asia

Introduction

Few westerners know much about Southeast Asia, beyond the fact that the Vietnam war was fought in the region. This region was, however, home to one of the world's earliest bronze-age societies (in northern Thailand). Rice cultivation appeared perhaps as early as 9,000 years before the modern era.

There is an immense number of races, cultures, and religions in this part of Asia. This mixture is emphasized and increased because the region serves as a link between China, India and the islands of the South Pacific. For example, early in its history, the state of Srivijaya played a major role in commercial contact between China and India. Moreover the region quickly became intergrated into global markets after the arrival of the Europeans This exercise introduces you to just a few of the cities and regions in Southeast Asia.

Locations

With different colored pencils, shade in and label the following cities or settlements and regions.

A. Cities

1. Batavia
2. Canton
3. Indrapura
4. Macao
5. Madras
6. Malacca
7. Manila

B. Regions

8. Angkor
9. Borneo
10. Champa
11. Mlaya
12. Nan Chao
13. Philippines
14. Srivijaya
15. Sumatra

Questions

Using a description of the geographical environment of the region, explain why Southeast Asia was never unified under a single government. What trade goods were most important to the economies of the region?

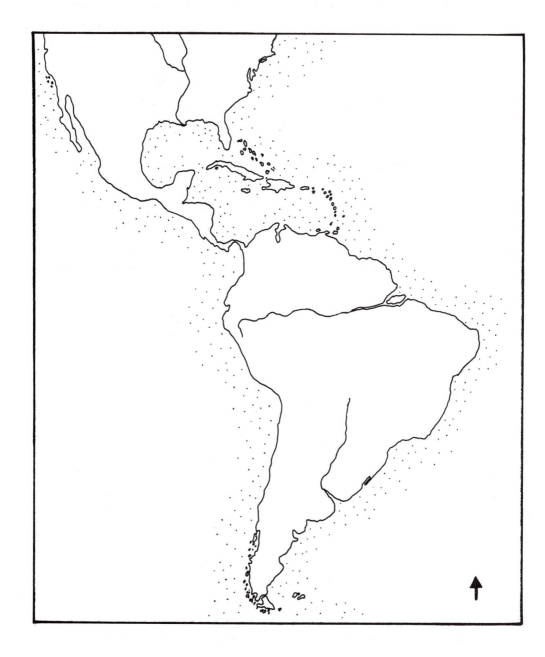

Exercise 23
European Conquests and Possessions in the West Indies

Introduction

In 1492 a new era in world history was launched. European adventurers took their ships in search of wealth, fame and new worlds to conquer and convert. These men provoked a transformation of Africa, Asia, the America's and Europe itself. This exercise looks at just one small part of the world affected by the European voyages and conquests.

Locations

With different colored pencils, shade in and number the following islands or regions and European spheres of influence

A. Islands or regions

1. Bahamas

2. Belize

3. Cuba

4. Florida

5. Jamaica

6. Lesser Antilles

7. Mosquito Coast

8. Puerto Rico

B. Spheres of influence

9. English areas

10. Spanish areas

Questions

What motivated European settlement in the West Indies? Discuss the short and long term impact of European settlement on the people and environment of the West Indies. What impact did the discovery of the West Indies have on the countries and people of Europe?

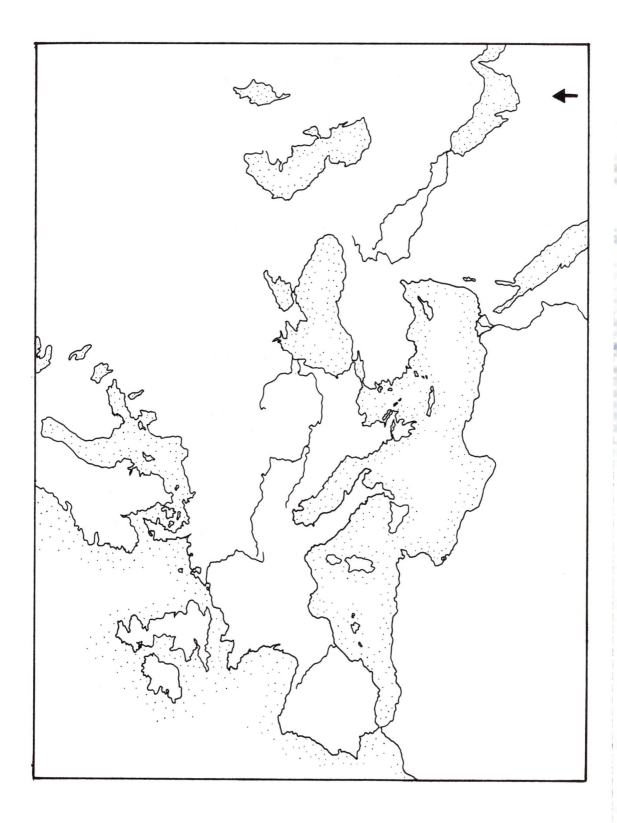

Exercise 24
Catholics and Protestants: 1550 CE

Introduction

In the sixteenth century abuses by the Catholic church, in particular the Papacy, were reaching a crisis point. Many reform movements grew out of the frustration of the times, some made surprisingly influential by the dissemination of these new ideas through the written word, now easily spread because of the printing press. The Reformation in Germany was to be one of the most influential. This particular reform movement was led by Martin Luther, the founder of Lutheranism. It was not long before the population of Europe had chosen sides: Protestant (e.g. Lutheran, Calvinist, Anglican) or Catholic. This exercise identifies some of the divisions, by religion, that appeared by the mid sixteenth century.

Locations

On your map, label the following cites and countries. Next to each number, write in the local religion (e.g. 1 - Roman Catholic).

A. Cities

1. Dijon
2. Dublin
3. Edinburgh
4. Lisbon
5. London
6. Munich

7. Paris
8. Rome
9. Seville
10. Trent

B. Countries

11. Denmark

12. Netherlands
13. Norway
14. Poland
15. Sweden

Questions

Compare and contrast the Reformation in England and Germany. Were the same reforming factors at work? Who initiated the Reformation in England? In Germany? What impact did the Reformation have on society in Europe? Give several examples.

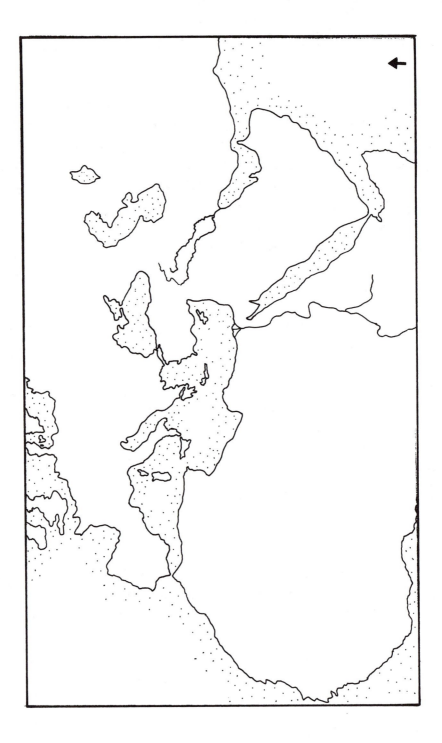

Exercise 25
The Turks and Their Neighbors

Introduction

Muslim empires dominated the Middle East and South Asia for several centuries. Despite European pressure, they brought stability to a traditionally unsettled region until the eighteenth century. By the end of the eighteenth century the powerful Ottoman Empire of the Turks had gradually begun to decline in power.

This exercise introduces you to the Middle East.

Locations

With different colored pencils, label the following cities, people, regions and geographical features and shade in the following imperial boundaries

A. Cities

1. Aleppo
2. Damascus
3. Isfahan
4. Istanbul
5. Salonica
6. Tabriz

B. People

7. Circassians

8. Uzbeks

C. Regions and geographical features

9. Aral Sea
10. Black Sea
11. Caspian Sea
12. Crimea
13. Euphrates River
14. Georgia

15. Mediterranean Sea
16. Morea
17. Najd
18. Persian Gulf

D. Boundaries

19. Ottoman empire (at its height)
20. Safavid empire (at its height)

Questions

What factors allowed the Ottomans to overthrow the Byzantine Empire in the 15th century? What factors finally limited the expansion of the Ottoman Empire into the Balkans? What are the main differences and similarities among the Moslem empires discussed in chapter 18?

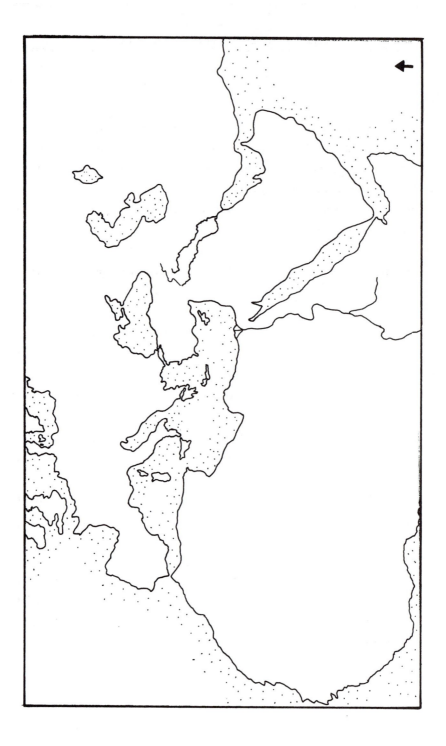

Exercise 26
The Ottoman Empire

Introduction

The Turkish people, led by the Ottomans, conquered the Byzantine Empire once and for all in 1453 with the capture of Constantinople. This was a tremendous victory and afterwards the Turks were on the move. They added vast tracts of lands to their wealthy empire.

The Ottomans were very effective at getting the Europeans to accept them as an equal power. They had a very intricate and effective government, with a strong and well organized military. This exercise traces the growth of Ottoman strength and influence in Europe and the Mediterranean regions.

Locations

With different colored pencils trace the boundaries of the Ottoman empire and locate the following regions and cities on your map.

A. Boundaries of the Ottoman empire	B. Regions	C. Cities
1. 1451	5. Anatolia	10. Cairo
2. 1481	6. Egypt	11. Athens
3. 1521	7. Syria	12. Belgrade
4. 1566	8. Transylvania	13. Damascus
	9. Wallachia	14. Istanbul
		15. Tunis

Questions

After 1566 the northern boundaries of the Ottoman empire were fairly fixed. What occurred to stop further movement in that direction? What were the strengths and weaknesses of the Ottomans? What were the long term results of their conquests?

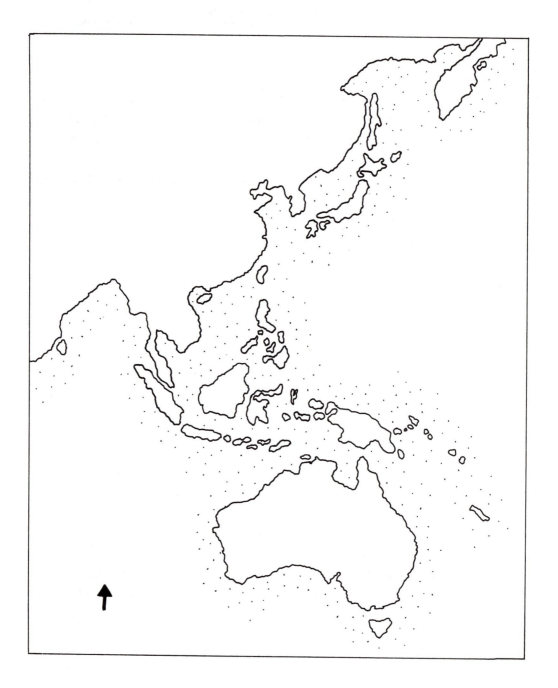

Exercise 27
East Asia: 1500-1800

Introduction

Vital new societies continued to develop in East Asia. Chinese and Japanese cultures earned the admiration and envy of neighbors and European observers. When the Portuguese first encountered the Chinese, this eastern civilization was the most advanced on earth.

In Japan, the 15th century ushered in an era of rivalries, but by the mid-16th century a process of unification had begun. Once in power, the dominant Tokugawa rulers initiated a long period of peace. This allowed economic growth and the flowering of Japanese cultural arts, such as literature, drama, pottery and painting.

Locations

With different colored pencils, place on your map the numbers of the following cities, then number and lightly shade in the regions and states.

A. Cities	8. Sakai	14. Guandong
1. Asano	9. Todo	15. Hunan
2. Beijing	10. Tsugaru	16. Inner Mongolia
3. Canton	11. Wuhan	17. Manchuria
4. Changsha		18. Sichuan
5. Hosokawa	**B. Regions and states**	19. Taiwan
6. Kuroda	12. Burma	20. Vietnam
7. Nanjing	13. Cambodia	

Questions

Describe the factors that led to the decline and fall of the Ming dynasty. Who were the Qing and how did they consolidate their power? List the states that participated in the tributary system of the Qing. What factors led to their incorporation into the system? Were they willing or unwilling participants?

What motivated the Japanese to isolate themselves from western cultures? Were they able to succeed?

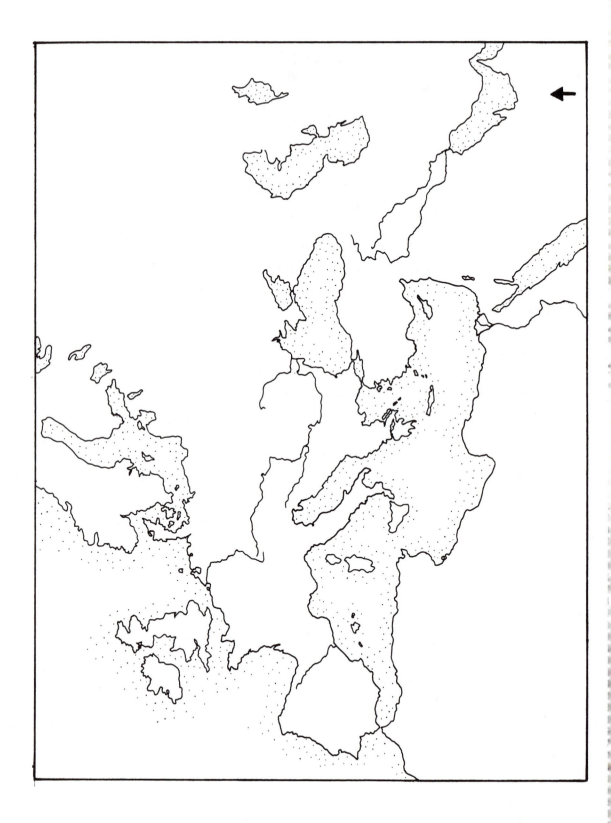

Exercise 28
The Enlightenment

Introduction

Because of the vast changes in communications, particularly the creation of the printing press, new ideas and trends spread faster than ever before. In the 18th century, four intellectual developments merged and were disseminated to create the revolutionary movement known as the Enlightenment. This exercise introduces you to some of the academic centers that were integral to the creation of the Enlightenment.

Locations

With different colored pencils locate the following centers of learning and publication.

A. Universities

1. Cambridge
2. Gottingen
3. Leiden

B. Publication sites

4. Amsterdam

5. Berlin
6. Florence
7. Geneva
8. London
9. Rome

C. Academic centers

10. Bologna
11. Copenhagen
12. Madrid
13. Turin
14. Uppsala
15. Venice

Questions

Describe the nature of the four intellectual developments. Name and discuss at least one important proponent of each of these.

What impact did the Enlightenment have on the debate about the nature and value of women? Who made the strongest case for the rights of women and what did this author write?

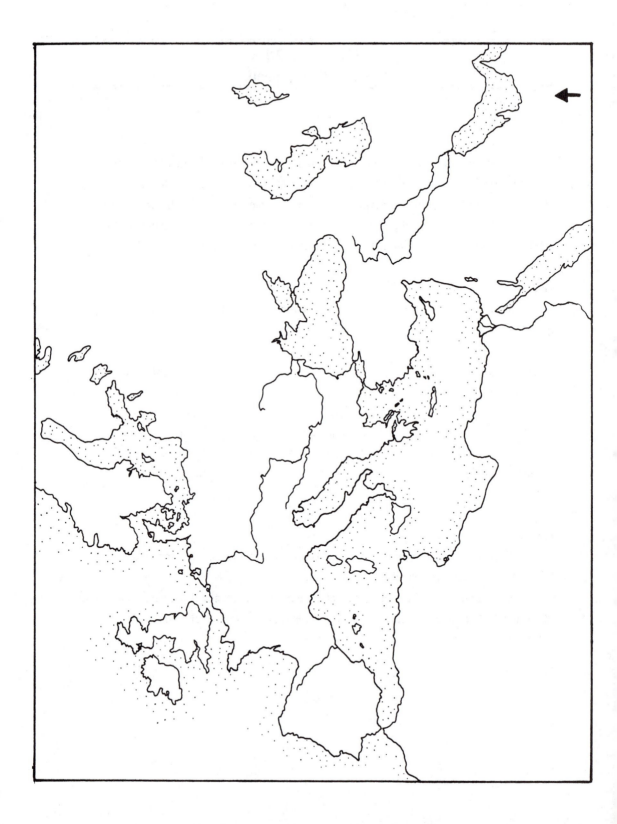

Exercise 29
Napoleon's Empire

Introduction

The late eighteenth century saw two important revolutions in the west: the American revolution and the French revolution. Both were the result of long term problems. The French sought, like the Americans, to ground their constitution in the idea of equal rights. The implementation of equal rights was neither easy nor peaceful. Other European nations feared that violent upheaval would spread from France and, thus, an informal coalition formed against the French. In response, the French had built up a large and impressive army and conquered even the Netherlands. Terror, instability and confusion soon dominated French politics and the economy. This situation allowed Napoleon to stage the coup d'état that would bring him to power. With his power he would try to create a long-lasting European empire, enlightened and fair. This exercise traces the growth of the Napoleonic state in Europe.

Locations

With colored pencils outline the boundaries of the French Empire under Napoleon then outline the boundaries of and place the number of the following neighboring territories. Next to the number, place the status of the territory with respect to the French Empire (eg., allied).

A. French Empire under Napoleon

1. Conferderacy of the Rhineland

2. Corsica

3. Grand Duchy of Warsaw

4. Imperial boundaries

5. Kingdom of Italy

6. Kingdom of Naples

7. Kingdom of Sicily

8. Sardinia

9. Saxony

10. Spain

Questions

What lands were gained by Napoleon? His was not a long lived empire. Why not? What factors ultimately led to his downfall? Generally what were the results of the revolutions of the eighteenth century? What were some of the major social, political, and territorial changes?

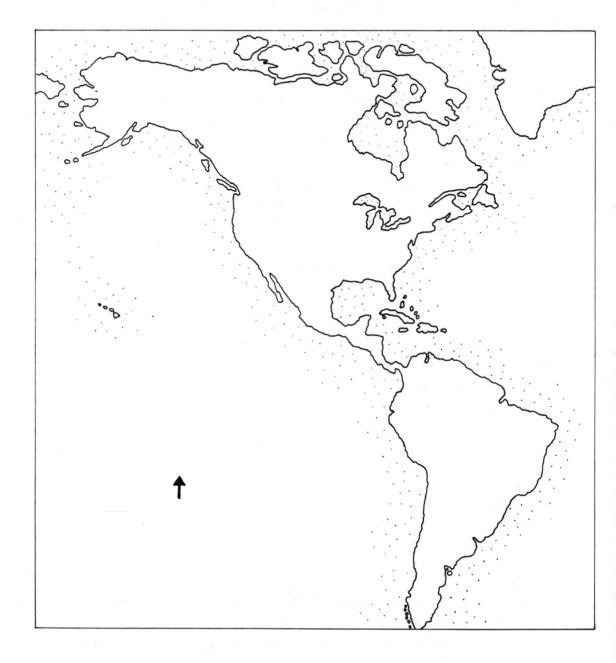

Exercise 30
Colonization and Independence in North America

Introduction

With the discovery of the Americas by the Europeans, a new era was begun. European powers claimed these territories for themselves, regardless of the original inhabitant's desires. Europeans brought with them a new way of life and old conflicts. It has taken hundreds of years to begin to sort out these conflicts fought on American soil.

This exercise introduces you to the European territories of North America.

Locations

On the map provided lightly shade in and number, using different colors, the following areas of European influences, control and colonies (by the 18th century), North American boundaries and the following cities and geographical features:

A. European influences, control and colonies

1. Dutch
2. English
3. French
4. Spanish

B. Boundaries

5. USA in 1803
6. USA in 1848
7. Canada in 1867
8. Canada in 1912

C. Cities

9. Boston
10. Chicago
11. Denver
12. New Orleans
13. New York
14. Philadelpnia
15. Quebec
16. San Francisco
17. Vancouver
18. Washington DC
19. Winnipeg

D. Geographical features

20. Colorado River
21. Great Lakes
22. Hudson Bay
23. Mississippi River
24. Missouri River
25. Rocky Mts.

Questions

In general, what happened to the societies found in North America by the European powers? How did the shifting boundaries, in particular, impact the native inhabitants? What explains European military successes over these societies?

By what means and for what reasons did the new USA free itself from British rule? How was this move similar and different from developments in Canada?

Extra Maps

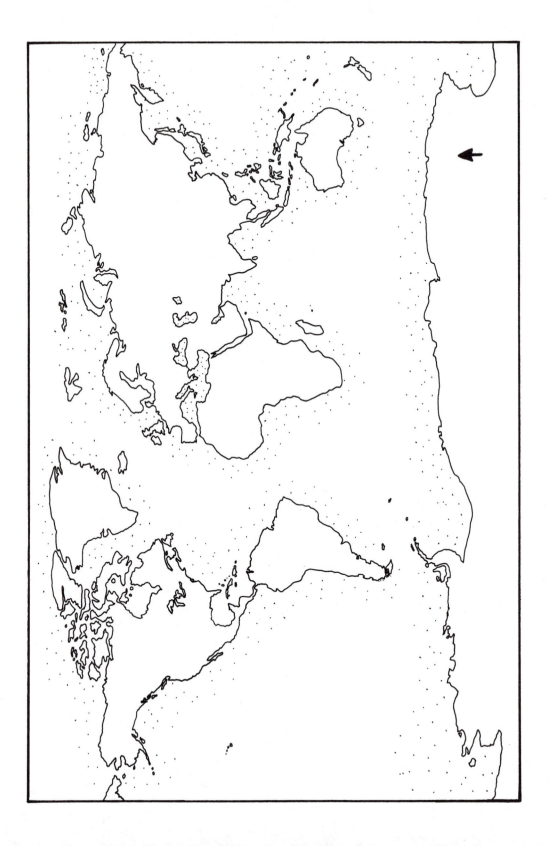

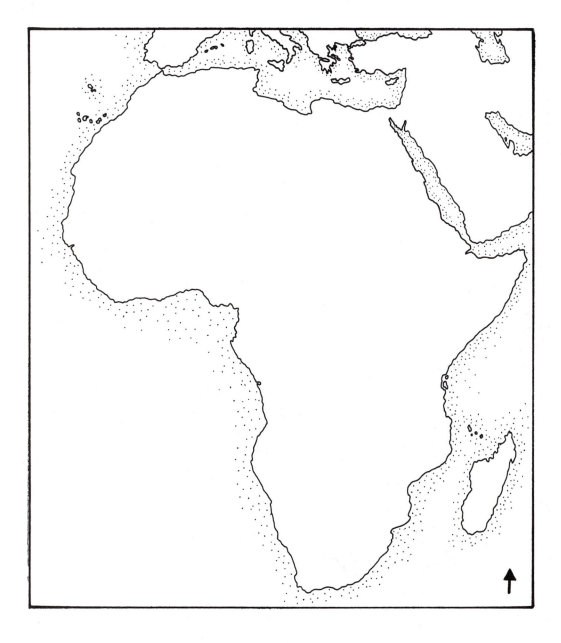

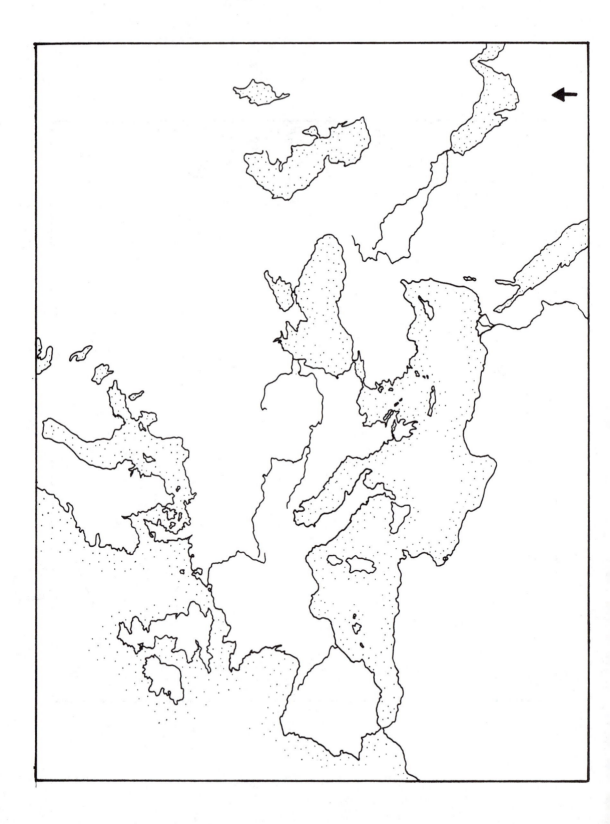

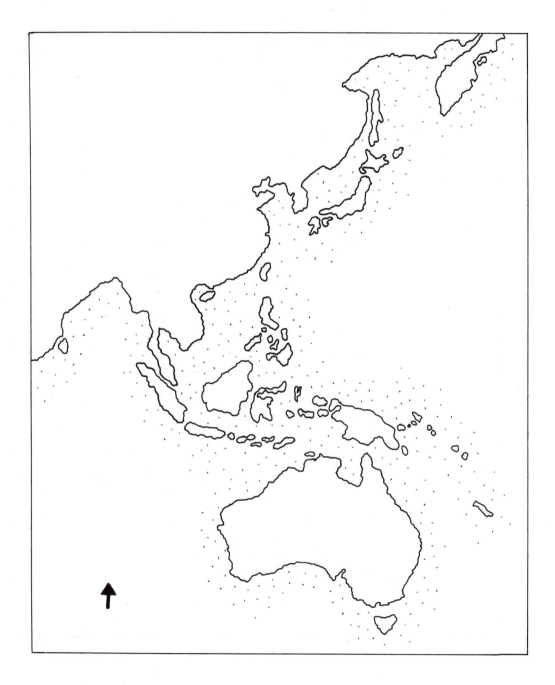

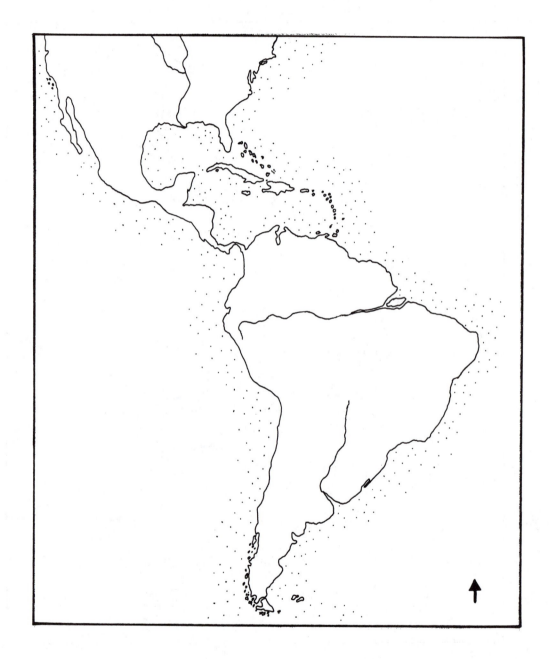

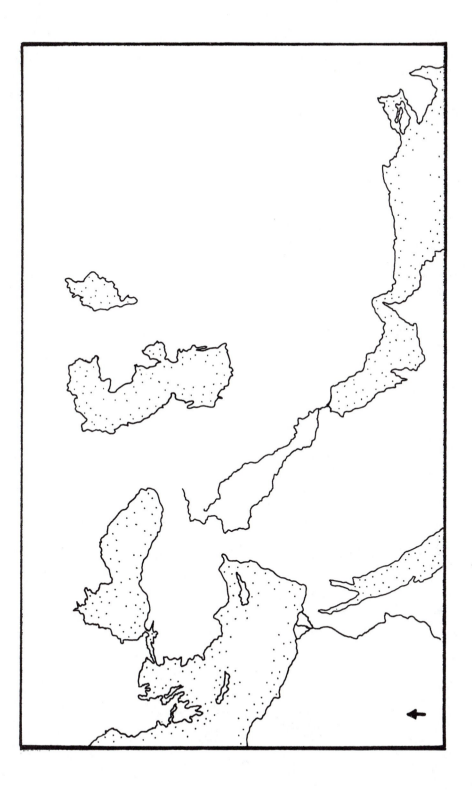